Weekly Units

Digital images courtesy of Getty's Open Content Program (page 32).
With thanks to Faye Buckingham (Advocate Art), Becky Miles, Susan Purcell,
Christos Skaltsas (Advocate Art), and Elaine Wilkinson.

A visit to the aquarium

Sasha and Josh are visiting an aquarium. "I want to see all the fish!" Josh shouts excitedly as he rushes in.

"Wow!" exclaims Sasha. "Look at that enormous fish tank!"

"Look at all the different fish," Josh whispers.

"I can see a shoal of red fish," says Sasha.

"I wish we could swim in there," says Josh.

Just then a big shark swims out of the shadows and across the tank. "Perhaps not," mutters Josh with a shiver.

Finally, they do some shopping. Sasha chooses a bag of shells and Josh gets a toy shark.

"He's fin-tastic," says Josh, cuddling his shark and smiling happily.

Read and draw

Circle the correct answer

Do the children visit a zoo?

Yes or No

Do they go swimming?

Yes or No

Do they see a shark?

Yes or No

Does Josh get a toy starfish?

Yes or No

What does Josh buy?

....

....

A day at the beach

Charlie and his family are at the beach.

"Let's hunt in the rock pools," suggests Charlie. They see some shrimps, three starfish, and a lot of shells. "Look," Charlie shouts, pointing to some seaweed. "I can see a little crab."

After a while, Charlie says, "I'm hot. Let's go for a swim."

After their swim, the family eat lunch. They have chicken sandwiches, crunchy carrot sticks, and chocolate chip cookies.

Then, the children build a huge sandcastle and decorate it with seashells, stones, seaweed, and some flags that Dad gave them.

Later, they dig a moat around the castle.

"That is such a grand castle," says Dad. "I wonder who lives there?"

Read and **draw**

a little crab

a flag

three starfish

a sandcastle

Circle the correct answer

Does the family visit a shopping mall? .... Yes or No

Do they see some shrimps? .... Yes or No

Does Charlie have cheese sandwiches? .... Yes or No

Do Charlie and his family go to the beach? .... Yes or No

What do the children dig around the sandcastle?

....

....

The three donkeys

Thor, Moth, and Thad are donkeys. They are looking hungrily at a patch of thistles.

The donkeys cannot reach the thistles, which are growing outside their paddock. "Thistles are our favorite," think all three donkeys.

Two children walk by. They stop and one asks, "What are the donkeys looking at?" The children look at the thistles.

"Yuck! It can't be those horrid prickly thistles," the other child replies.

"We'll find you some nice fresh grass," the children say to the donkeys.

The donkeys look at the children and then back to the lovely, yummy thistles and think...

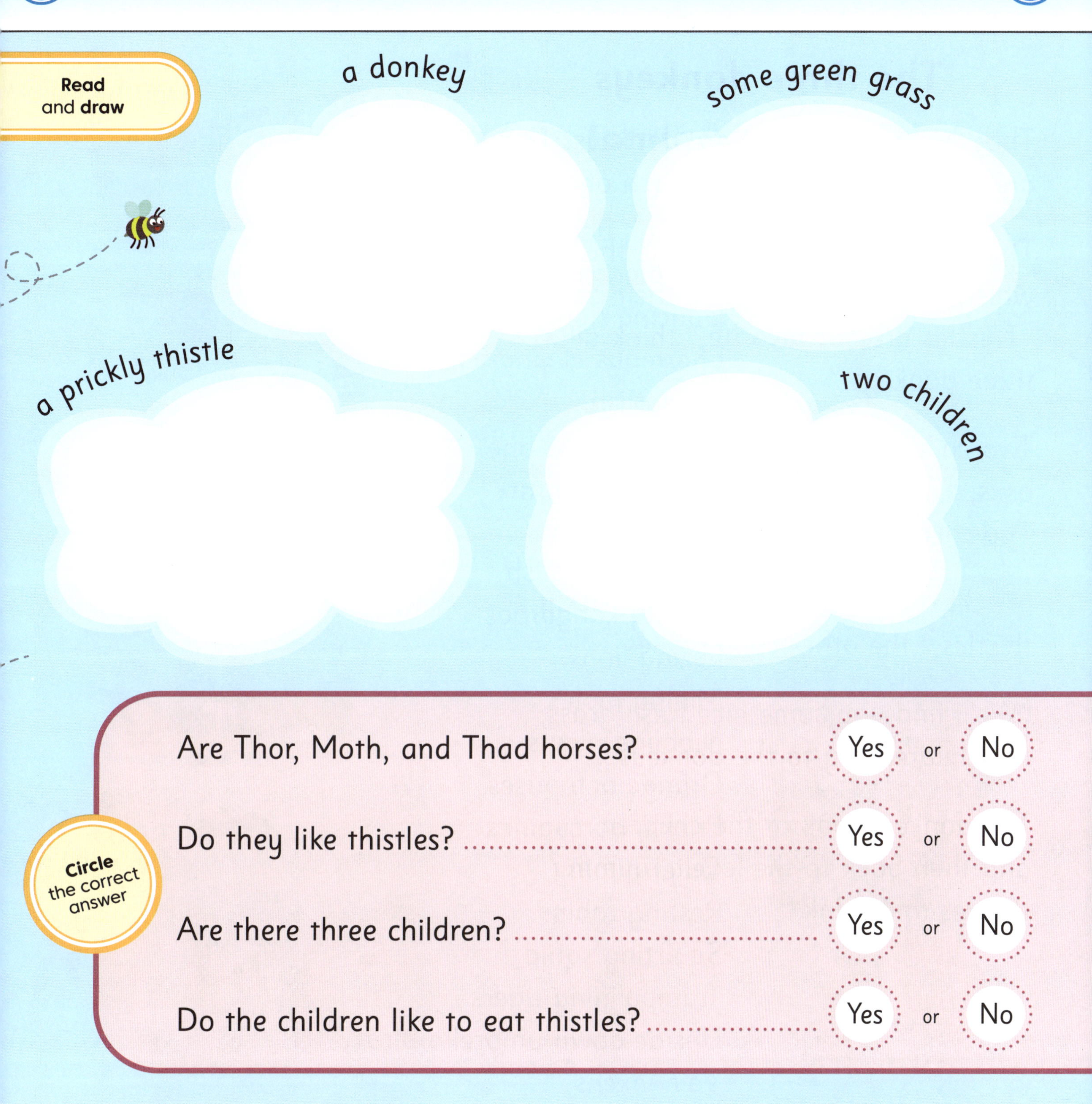

Are Thor, Moth, and Thad horses? .... Yes or No

Do they like thistles? .... Yes or No

Are there three children? .... Yes or No

Do the children like to eat thistles? .... Yes or No

What do the donkeys like to eat?

....

....

Animal alphabet

Angry ants
Buzzing bees
Clapping cats
Dancing donkeys
Enormous elephants
Flying fish
Grumpy goats
Hiccuping hippos
Itching insects
Jumping jellyfish
Kicking kangaroos
Lazing lions
Mining moles
Nibbling newts
Orange octopuses
Prickly porcupines
Quiet quails
Resting robins
Squirting squid
Trampolining tigers
Upside-down umbrella birds
Vain vixens
Waddling wombats
Boxing foxes
Yelling yaks
Zigzagging zebras
...at my zoo!

Read and **draw**

an orange octopus

boxing foxes

flying fish

a trampolining tiger

Are the bees buzzing?

Yes or No

Are the squid singing?

Yes or No

Are the wombats wiggling?

Yes or No

Are the newts nibbling?

 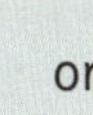 

Yes or No

What other -ing words could describe what a tiger might do?

....

....

An Australian animal park

Dear Granny and Grandpa,

Yesterday, we went to an Australian animal park. We saw lots of kangaroos and some wombats.

I liked the quokkas best. They look as if they are smiling all the time. We saw numbats. They have long sticky tongues to catch ants. We also saw some duck-billed platypuses swimming in a tank.

Then we went to the "Meet the Animals" talk. We saw a koala and her baby, and I stroked a giant millipede. No one else would touch it!

See you soon, Zack.

Mrs and Mrs Cliff
280 Main Street
Springfield
Texas
78553

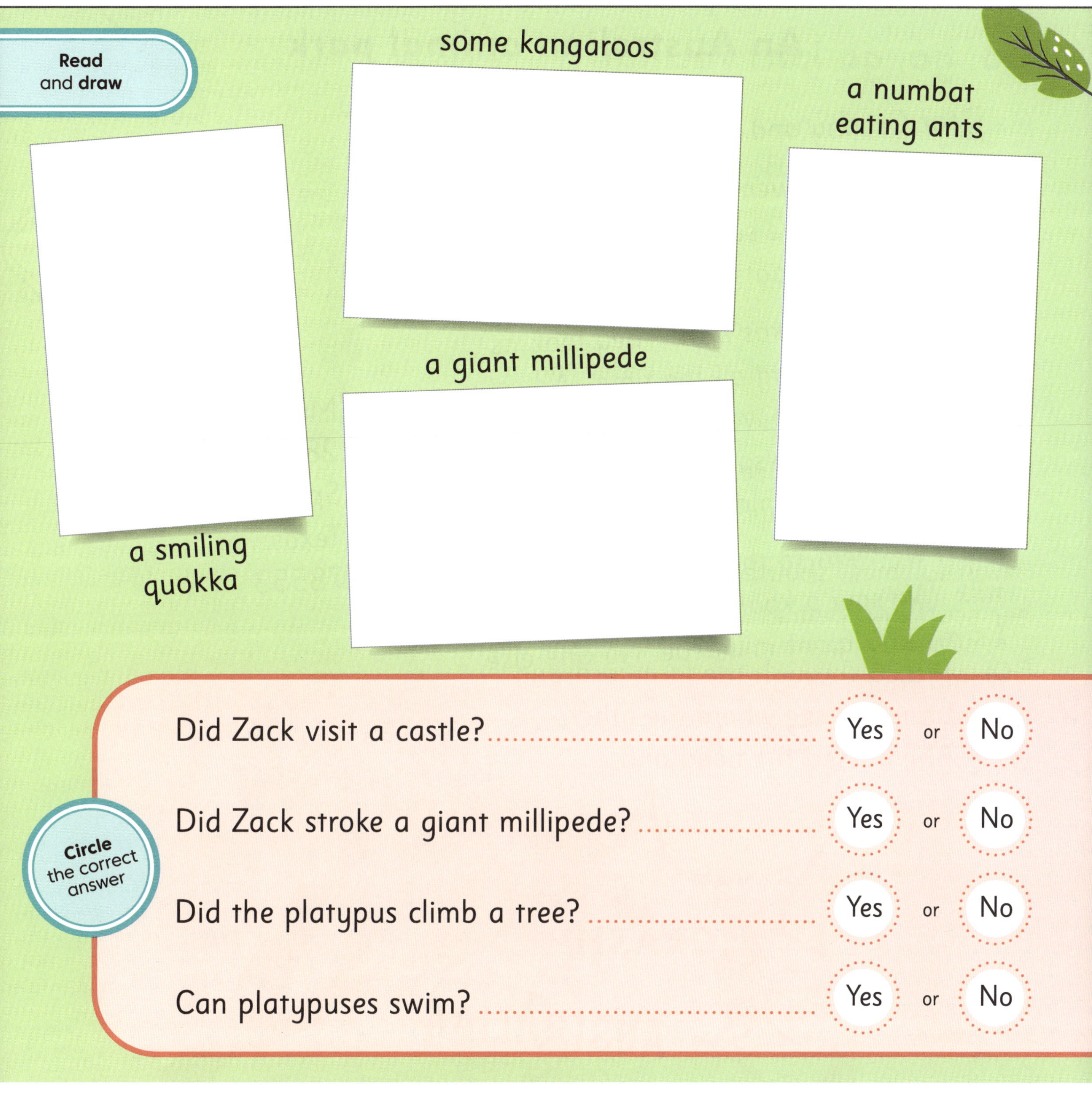

Who did Zack send a postcard to?

....

....

Go, go, go-kart racing!

Inky, Bee, and Snake had made go-karts for the Soap Box Derby race.

"Let's try them out on the farm track," suggested Bee.

At the start of the track, Bee waved and cried, "Byeeeeee!" as she shot off down the hill.

"I'll catch you up, Bee. Your go-kart moves like a slug!" yelled Snake.

"Wait for me!" shouted Inky, putting on her scarf and helmet.

Bee whizzed through the farmyard and looked back to see where the others were. She missed the bend and...

...CRASH!

Snake and Inky rushed to help Bee. Her go-kart was on its side.

"Ouch!" Bee cried. "I was whizzing along and suddenly the go-kart flipped over. I hit the ground hard, but I'm all right."

Read and draw

Snake wearing a helmet.

a slug

Inky with a scarf.

Bee in a go-kart.

Circle the correct answer

Had Inky, Bee, and Snake made boats? .... Yes or No

Did Bee's go-kart crash? .... Yes or No

Did Snake's go-kart flip over? .... Yes or No

Why did Bee crash?

....

....

Write three common nouns from the story:

....

My week

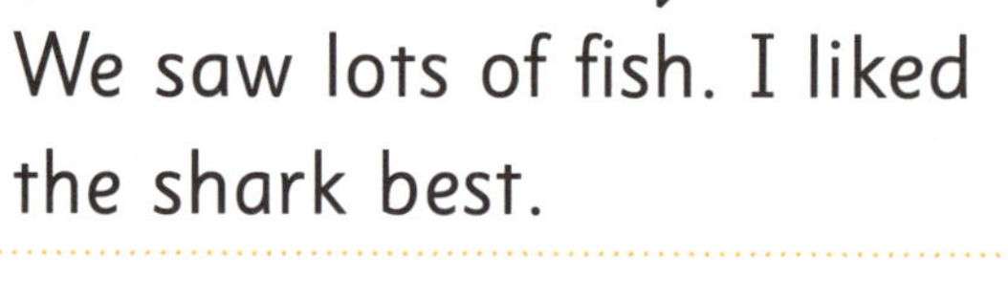

Monday	We went to an aquarium. We saw lots of fish. I liked the shark best.
Tuesday	At Grandma's, we made banana bran muffins. Grandma's dog hoped he would get some!
Wednesday	We fed the ducks in the park. The squirrels tried to steal some corn, but the ducks quacked loudly and flapped their wings.
Thursday	I had a swimming lesson. I jumped in and swam a length of the pool for the first time.
Friday	I went to a farm park with my friend Harper. We played with some little goats and I got a postcard of them.
Saturday	I went to Zack's party at the ball park. We had cheese sandwiches and chocolate cake.
Sunday	I helped Dad cook a roast dinner. I peeled the vegetables and chopped some apples to make a pie for dessert.

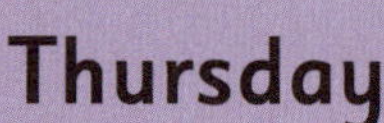

Activity

Read and **draw**

three ducks on the pond

a squirrel in a tree

Circle the correct answer

Did the family visit Grandma on Monday? .... Yes or No

Did they feed the ducks on Wednesday? .... Yes or No

Did they have apple pie on Friday? .... Yes or No

What sort of muffins did they bake with Grandma on Tuesday?

....

....

What day was Zack's party?

....

....

Puffins

Puffins are small black and white birds with colorful beaks. They have red and black eye markings and bright orange legs. They are sometimes called sea parrots.

Puffins nest in small burrows in cliffs and usually lay just one egg. A young puffin is called a puffling. Puffin parents stay together for life.

Puffins catch fish and sand eels by diving into the water and "swimming" with their wings and feet. They can carry lots of fish in their beaks.

In August, the adults fly out to sea and leave the pufflings. The pufflings have to make their own way to the water when they are six or seven weeks old.

Puffins spend the winter far out to sea before returning to the same nests in spring.

Common name:
Atlantic or common puffin

Scientific name:
Fratercula arctica
/f-r-a-t-er-k-ue-l-a ar-k-t-i-k-a/

Height: 18–25 cm

Wingspan: 47–63 cm

Range: North Atlantic (from Canada and the United States to Iceland, Norway, and as far south as Spain).

Read and **draw**

a puffin

Are puffins big birds?

Yes or No

Do they nest in burrows?

Yes or No

Do puffins eat beetles and insects?

Yes or No

Is a baby puffin called a muffling?

Yes or No

What color are the eye markings and legs of a puffin?

....

....

Where do puffins spend the winter?

....

....

Is this writing fiction or nonfiction?

....

Hickory dickory dock

Hickory dickory dock,
The mouse ran up the clock.
The clock struck one,
The mouse ran down,
Hickory dickory dock—tick tock!

Hickory dickory dock,
The mouse ran up the clock.
The clock struck two,
The mouse cried, "Yahoo!"
And floated down from the clock—tick tock!

Hickory dickory dock,
The mouse ran up the clock.
The clock struck three,
The mouse yelled, "Wheeeee!"
And swung to and fro on the clock—tick tock!

Hickory dickory dock,
The mouse ran up the clock.
The clock struck four,
The mouse ran to the door,
Hickory dickory dock—tick tock!

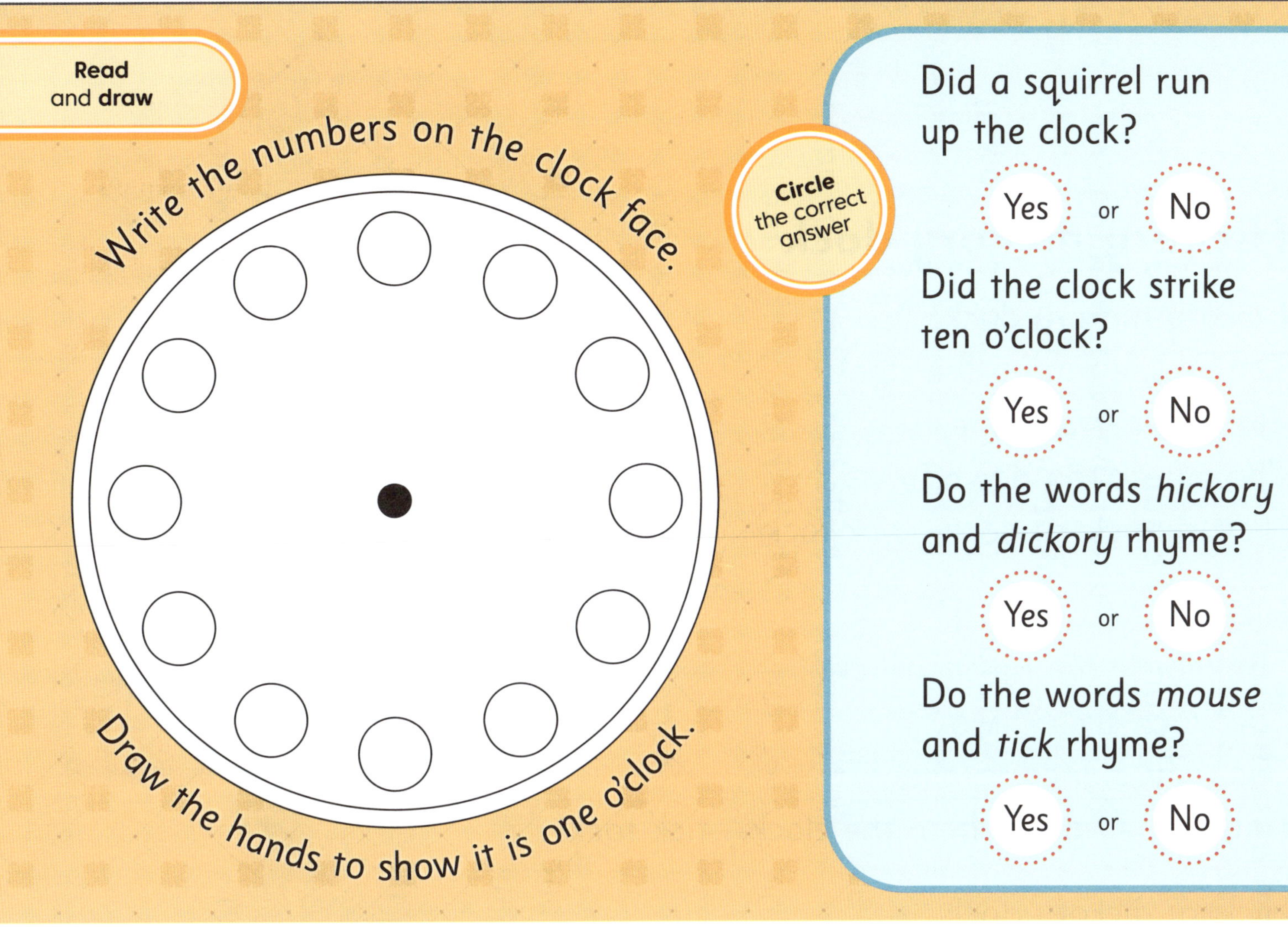

Circle the correct answer

Did a squirrel run up the clock?

Yes or No

Did the clock strike ten o'clock?

Yes or No

Do the words *hickory* and *dickory* rhyme?

Yes or No

Do the words *mouse* and *tick* rhyme?

Yes or No

What did the mouse do first?

....

What did the mouse do at two o'clock?

....

Which words from the verses rhyme with these words?

two .... three .... four ....

Find words in the rhyme that begin with these letters:

cl............................ sw............................ cr............................

The Wind and the Sun

Narrator: The Wind…

Wind: **(Puffs and blows loudly.)**

Narrator: …and the Sun…

Sun: **(Smiles, showing open hands either side of face.)**

Narrator: …were having an argument.

Wind: I am so strong!

Narrator: …shouted the Wind, making the windmill's sails spin around.

Sun: **(Smiling and shaking head.)** No, I don't think so.

Narrator: Just then, the Wind saw someone wearing a big coat walking uphill.

Person: **(Walks slowly across stage, then stops and looks around.)**

Wind: I will show you I am stronger!

Narrator: …boasted the Wind.

Wind: **(Starts blowing and blowing.)** I will blow that coat away!

Narrator: The Wind blew and blew but…

Person: **(Person shivers and huddles under the coat, holding the collar tightly.)** Brrrrr!

Narrator: …the coat did not blow away.

Sun: **(Smiling, showing open hands either side of face.)** My turn…

Narrator: …smiled the Sun. It got hotter…

Person: **(Wipes brow with hand.)** It's getting hot.

Narrator: …and hotter. It was much too hot to wear such a big coat.

Person: **(Takes off coat and walks off.)** I'm too hot.

Narrator: The Wind stormed off…

Wind: **(Waves arms, blowing and huffing, and stomps off, looking grumpy.)**

Narrator: …and the Sun continued to smile and shine.

Sun: **(Smiles.)**

Read and **draw**

Draw the Wind with an angry face. Color it blue.
Draw the Sun with a happy face. Color it yellow.

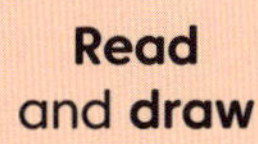

Circle the correct answer

Did it get warmer when the Sun shone? .... Yes or No

Did the Wind win the argument? .... Yes or No

Did the person take off a hat? .... Yes or No

Was the Sun angry? .... Yes or No

Why did the person take off their coat? ....

....

What did the Wind do in the end? ....

....

What makes you happy, like the Sun? ....

....

The Wind and the Sun

The Wind liked to think he was very strong. He enjoyed seeing the trees and grass sway when he was tearing about.

One day, he met the Sun. "Wow!" he cried as he puffed clouds across the Sun's face. "I am stronger than you!" he howled.

"I don't think you are," glinted the Sun, smiling.

"Rrrubbbishhhh! See that man down there wearing that big coat? I bet I can blow it off him," the Wind boasted.

"Go on then," said the Sun.

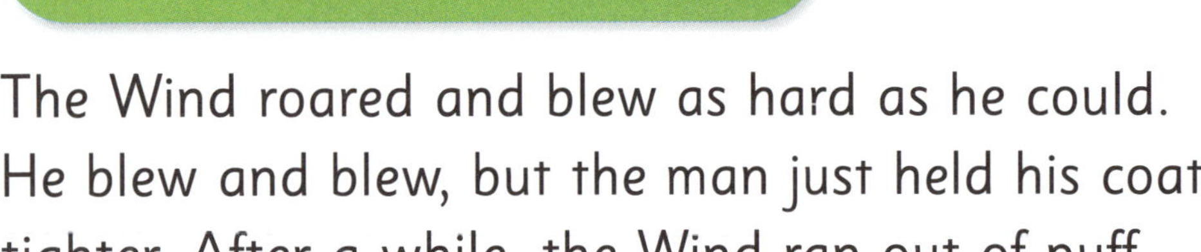

The Wind roared and blew as hard as he could. He blew and blew, but the man just held his coat tighter. After a while, the Wind ran out of puff.

"My turn," flashed the Sun. As the Sun smiled, the air got hotter. As it got hotter, the man shrugged off his coat. "There!" twinkled the Sun.

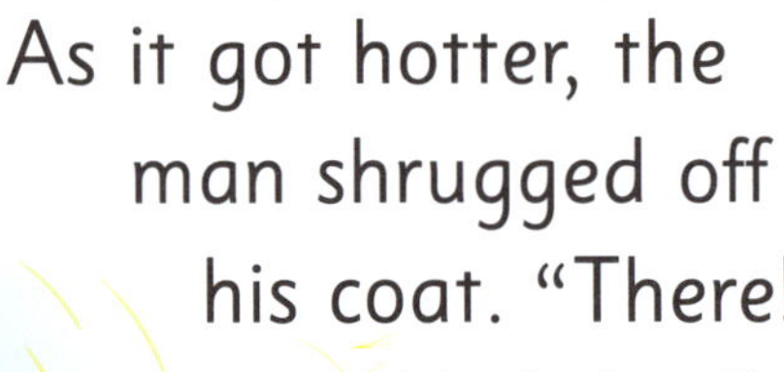

The Wind was so angry he stormed off in a big huff.

Read and **draw**

The Sun smiling as the Wind blows the man, the trees, and the flowers.

Write inside the letters and punctuation in the sentence:

"Brrr! It's cold," said the man.

Circle the correct answer

Did it get hotter when the Wind blew? .... Yes or No

Did the Wind like blowing things around? .... Yes or No

Did the Sun boast that she was stronger? .... Yes or No

Was the Wind angry? .... Yes or No

What did the Wind like doing? ....

....

Why did the Wind stop blowing? ....

....

Flower farm

Next to a farmhouse was a big square field. Sally, Farmer Green's wife, stood and looked at the bare area.

Sally wanted to start her own little flower farm there. She prepared the ground and divided it into squares. Then, into each square she planted some different flower seeds. "That will do," she said.

Next, she made a scarecrow and stood it in the middle of the field. "There!" she said.

She cared for the seeds, and by the summer they had all grown so the field was full of squares of different colored flowers. There were yellow sunflowers, white daisies, pink cosmos, purple lavender, blue delphiniums, and orange marigolds.

"A rainbow of flowers," said Sally, as she made them up into colorful bunches to sell at the farmers' market.

Read and **draw**

a scarecrow

a bunch of flowers

Circle the correct answer

Did Sally want to grow vegetables? .... Yes or No

Did she make a scarecrow? .... Yes or No

Were the flowers planted in squares? .... Yes or No

Were the flowers all the same color? .... Yes or No

What did Sally want to grow? ....

....

What did she do with the flowers? ....

....

Why did she make a scarecrow? ....

....

Grandpa's party

Holly's grandfather was having a party.

On Saturday morning, Holly helped lay out the food and set up a big red tent and some games in the garden. All the family were coming to the party.

By lunchtime, everyone was very hungry. Holly's dad was cooking food on the barbecue. Suddenly it started to rain.

"Quickly!" shouted Holly's dad. "Bring me an umbrella. The food is getting wet."

Uncle Jimmy ran over and held an umbrella over the barbecue.

After lunch, the rain stopped, so they could leave the tent and play all the games outside.

That evening, Grandpa was very happy. "I did enjoy my party," he said. "It was a really fantastic day, even if it was a bit wet," he chuckled.

Read and **draw**

an umbrella

a red tent

Write inside the letters and punctuation in the sentence:

"Quickly!" shouted Holly's dad.

Circle the correct answer

Was the party for Holly?

Yes or No

Did Holly's dad cook?

Yes or No

Did it rain?

Yes or No

Was the party on Friday?

Yes or No

What happened when it started to rain?

....

....

What kind of food would you eat at a party?

....

....

A thank-you cake

Jane lives next door to old Mrs Baker. One rainy evening, Jane looked out of her window and saw Mrs Baker trip on the sidewalk and fall over. Jane shouted for her mom and they ran out to help.

The next day, they went to see Mrs Baker and took her a bunch of grapes. She had a cut on her nose and a black eye.

The next weekend, Mrs Baker came round carrying a huge ginger cake with Jane's name on it.

"I made it for you and used chocolate stars to decorate it," said Mrs Baker, "because you were such a star for helping me."

Now, Mrs Baker often visits Jane and her mom, and brings them cakes.

"I enjoy visiting. I'm glad something good came out of my fall," she said, and smiled.

Read and **draw**

a bunch of grapes

a cake with chocolate stars

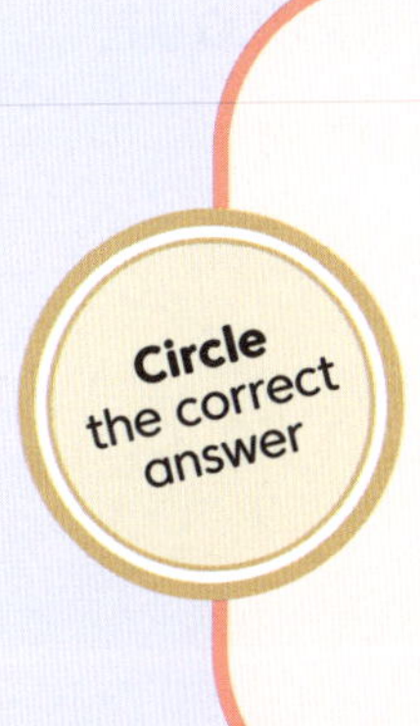

Did Mrs Baker trip over?

Yes or No

Did she cut her nose?

Yes or No

Did she hurt her arm?

Yes or No

Did she make a ginger cake?

Yes or No

Why did Mrs Baker fall over? ....

....

Why did she make a cake for Jane? ....

....

How did Mrs Baker decorate the cake? ....

....

What is your favorite sort of cake? ....

....

Anansi the spider and the melon

One morning, Anansi the spider made a hole in Goat's prize melon with a thorny spike. The spider squeezed inside and ate as much of the melon as he could. But when it was time to climb out he was stuck!

"I'll have to stay," he smiled.

The next day, Goat picked the melon. "Hey!" shouted Anansi.

"Wow, a talking melon!" gasped Goat. "I must take it to the king."

The king ordered the melon to speak, but it didn't.

"Silly!" said the king.

"Excuse me!" replied Anansi from inside. "You are the one talking to a melon!"

The king was so cross, he threw the melon out of the window. It smashed and Anansi crawled out. He ran up a tree and hid in a bunch of bananas.

"That's the last time I listen to a melon," cried Goat.

"No, you can never trust a melon," replied a banana.

Read and **draw**

Anansi the spider

the king and Goat

Circle the correct answer

Is Anansi a goat?

Yes or No

Does Anansi like playing tricks?

Yes or No

Did Anansi make a hole in a pumpkin?

Yes or No

Was the king cross when the melon didn't speak?

Yes or No

Why did Anansi make a hole in the melon? ....

....

Why was Anansi stuck in the melon?...

....

Why was the king cross? ....

....

Globes

In years gone by, people thought that the world was flat. They didn't know it was round like a ball or a sphere.

A globe is a model of the planet and shows how it looks from space. On a globe you can see the land and seas. It can also show countries, cities, mountains, rivers, and lakes.

You can turn a globe to see how the Earth rotates. Then, use a flashlight to show where it is day and night.

Globes have been made for hundreds of years. When some places were unexplored and people didn't know what was there, they would draw pictures onto maps and globes of imaginary animals, like dragons and monsters.

Digital image courtesy of Getty's Open Content Program.

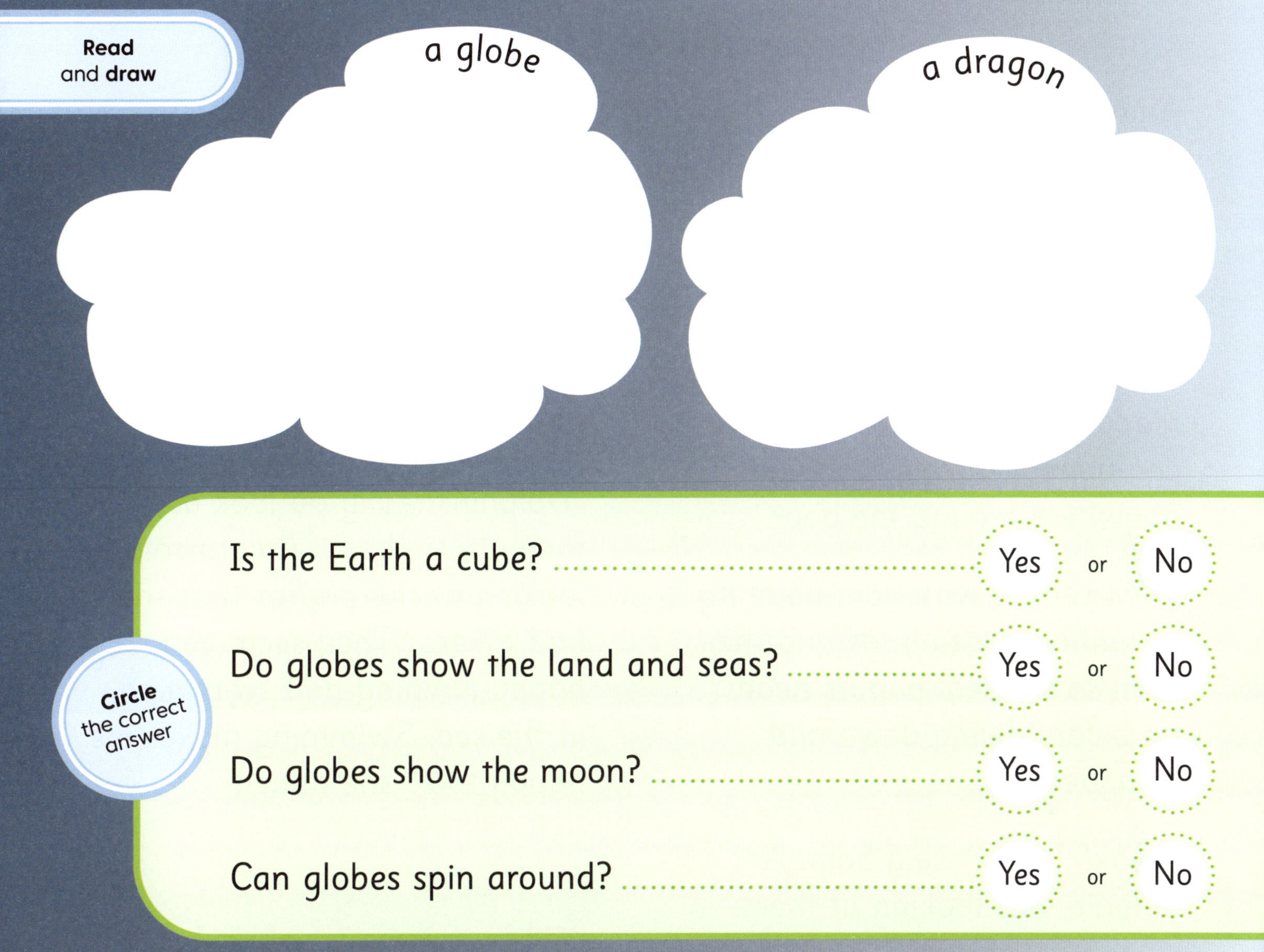

What shape is a globe? ....

....

What does a globe show? ....

....

Why did people draw dragons or monsters on maps? ....

....

Boat trip

Amara and Hammad were going on a dolphin-spotting boat trip. When they arrived, Sam the captain gave them life jackets to put on.

"Keep your phones and cameras ready," he said. "The dolphins can appear at any time and anywhere around the boat."

They set off, with Sam pointing out different sea birds and they even saw a seal pop its head up before diving down and disappearing.

"Look! There!" said Sam. A dolphin was looking at them.

Amara quickly took some photographs. Two other dolphins appeared and swam alongside the boat for a little bit.

"That was brilliant!" exclaimed Hammad when they got back to land.

"Dolphins really do look as if they are smiling," Amara said, looking at the photos that she had taken. "They seem very happy jumping and swimming in the sea. Swimming makes me happy too," she added.

Read and **draw**

a dolphin

Amara and Hammad on a boat

Circle the correct answer

Did they go on an elephant-spotting trip? ...... Yes or No

Was the captain of the boat called Sam? .... Yes or No

Did they see ten dolphins? .... Yes or No

Did Amara take some photographs? .... Yes or No

What animal were they hoping to see? ....

....

What other creatures did they see? ....

....

Why did Amara think the dolphins were happy? ....

....

How the whale got his throat

Once there was a greedy whale. He ate and ate until there was only one fish left in the whole sea!

This fish was clever.

"Oh Whale, have you ever tasted a person?" he whispered. "People are yummy, and over there is a shipwrecked sailor on a raft."

Whale swam, opened his mouth and swallowed the sailor, raft, and all. Inside the whale, the sailor kicked and punched.

"This sailor is making me hiccup," complained Whale.

Inside, the sailor yelled, "Take me home or I'll keep making you hiccup!"

Whale swam to where the man lived and opened his mouth. Out climbed the man, whistling happily, but he left the raft stuck in the whale's throat.

From then on, the raft stopped Whale from eating anything except very tiny fish.

Read and **draw**

a whale

a little fish

a sailor on a raft

Circle the correct answer

Is a whale small? .... Yes or No

Did the whale eat all the seaweed? .... Yes or No

Was the sailor on a raft? .... Yes or No

Why was the sailor on a raft? ....

....

Why did the whale take the sailor home? ....

....

Why couldn't the whale eat big fish any more? ....

....

Book Week

Miss Beech's class was excited because it was Book Week. The children were looking forward to reading lots of new books and having some different lessons.

Today, there was also going to be a book sale. A display of books had been set up in the hall, and after recess the class went in to look at all the books.

"Yay!" Anna pointed to a book with a unicorn on the cover. "I love books about unicorns and horses," she said.

"Great!" exclaimed Seth excitedly, as he picked up a book. "I haven't read this one. Sam Hay is my favorite author. I've read all his Little Dragon series."

May stood and looked around. "So many books," she whispered. "I'm going to write a book one day," she promised herself.

Read and **draw**

a little dragon

a unicorn

Circle the correct answer

Was it Table Week?

Yes or No

Was there going to be a book sale?

Yes or No

Does Anna like unicorns?

Yes or No

Does May want to be an author?

Yes or No

What had been set up in the hall? ....

....

Why was Seth happy? ....

....

What does an author do? ....

....

Characters

The children had enjoyed reading lots of stories during Book Week, and today they were each dressed up as characters from stories or rhymes.

Hinda was Miss Muffet with a bowl, teaspoon, and a toy spider. "I really am scared of spiders," she whispered.

Seth was Robin Hood with a toy bow and arrow. "I am brave and strong," he boasted.

Rob was a wizard with a spell book and a wooden wand. He kept pointing the wand and shouting, "Kazoom!"

"ROAR!" Gus cried, as he stomped along. "I am a huge, scary, fire-breathing dragon!"

Anna was Anansi the spider. She had attached six extra-long legs to her T-shirt, giving her eight legs in all. "Look out! I am very tricky," Anna chuckled.

Bill was pretending to be Jack, and he had made a beanstalk from a cane, with green paper leaves and real beans.

Read and **draw**

Jack and his beanstalk

a scary, fire-breathing dragon

Circle the correct answer

Were the children dressing up?

Yes or No

Did Hinda have a toy dog?

Yes or No

Was Gus dressed as a unicorn?

Yes or No

Did Bill make a beanstalk?

Yes or No

Which character was Anna? ....

....

What sort of dragon was Gus? ....

....

What had Bill put on his beanstalk? ....

....

The night sky

Inky, Snake, and Bee were looking up at the night sky. They had found a high spot, away from lights, so the stars were bright.

Earlier, Phonic had explained to them that people long ago thought they could see shapes and pictures in the stars.

"Sets of stars are called constellations," Phonic said, and showed them a picture of the Great Bear on his screen. "See if you can spot this constellation tonight."

"There's the Great Bear!" said Inky, later that night. "Travelers and sailors used to use stars to find their way before there were roads and signposts."

"I'm hoping to see some shooting stars," sighed Bee. "Shooting stars aren't really stars," said Snake. "They're bits of rock falling into Earth's atmosphere and burning up."

"Well, I still like to think of them as shooting stars," replied Bee.

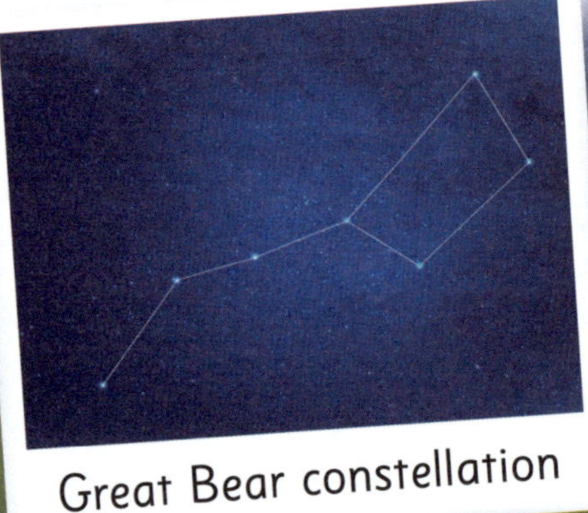

Great Bear constellation

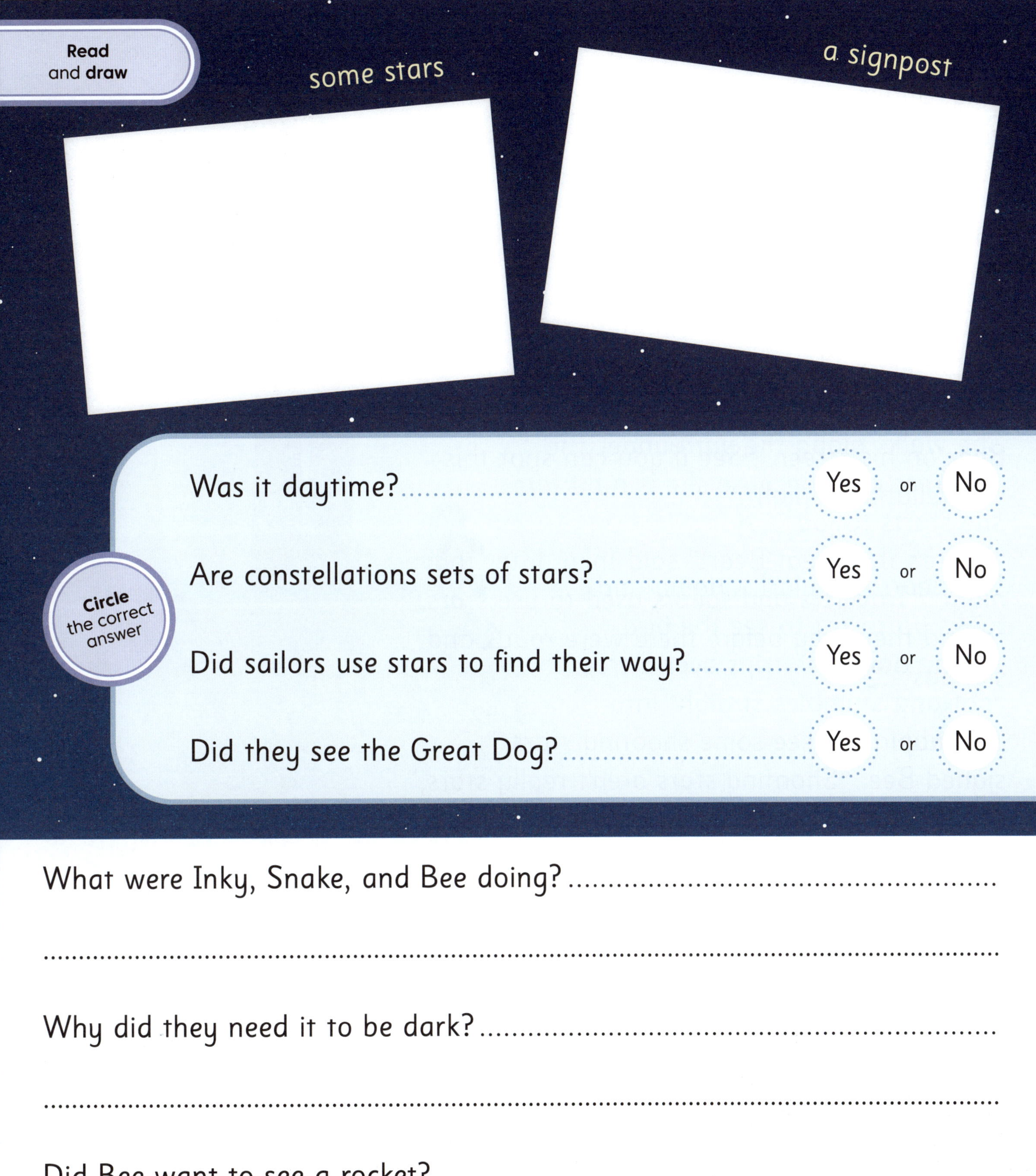

Was it daytime? .... Yes or No

Are constellations sets of stars? .... Yes or No

Did sailors use stars to find their way? .... Yes or No

Did they see the Great Dog? .... Yes or No

What were Inky, Snake, and Bee doing? ....

....

Why did they need it to be dark? ....

....

Did Bee want to see a rocket? ....

....

Monster party

Out of a dark cave steps a shy monster, with a hairy, green body, webbed toes, and two beady, bright eyes. In her hand she holds a gift tied with a shiny ribbon.

The monster smiles, showing pointed, white teeth. She is happy because she is going to her friend's birthday party. She walks along the path under the tall trees and, because she is a bit late, she starts to jog.

She hears a skylark singing and looks up to try to see the bird. As she does, she trips over a tree root and stumbles straight into a muddy pond!

She sits up. Now she is a muddy, soggy, smelly, green monster.

"No need to go home and get dry," she cries. "I look perfect for a monster party!"

Read and **draw**

a hairy, green monster

A muddy, hairy, green monster in a pond.

Circle the correct answer

Is the cave light? .... Yes or No

Does the monster have webbed toes? .... Yes or No

Is she happy? .... Yes or No

Where does the monster live? ....

....

Why does she start to run? ....

....

Why does she think she is perfect for the party after falling in the pond?

....

....

The abominable snowman

It had been snowing, so Inky, Snake, and Bee were building a snowman.

"I don't want to make just any snowman. I want to make our own abominable snowman!" Snake cried.

They piled up snow until they had a huge mound. Then, they made a head and used two yellow tennis balls for eyes. They gave the snowman long arms with elbows and big feet.

"He really does look abominable," squeaked Inky.

That night before going to bed, Inky looked out of the window. In the dark, the snowflakes swirled around, making it difficult to see. She squinted. Where was their abominable snowman?

She quickly put on her coat and boots and went outside. Big, snowy footprints led away, across the garden and into the darkness. Their abominable snowman had gone!

Read and **draw**

Inky, Bee and Snake making the abominable snowman.

Circle the correct answer

Did Inky, Bee and Snake make a snowman?

Yes or No

Was it a snowy day?

Yes or No

Did they use red tennis balls for the snowman's eyes?

Yes or No

Were the footprints very big?

Yes or No

What was the weather like? ....

....

What sort of snowman did Snake want to make? ....

....

What did Inky find when she went outside that night? ....

....

Monster Times

Abominable Sight

Reporter: Jim Chew

There have been reports of a massive abominable snowman in the local area. Sets of enormous footprints have been found in the snow.

"When I went out last night I could see huge footprints across my garden," said Inky Mouse.

Police were also called to Hillside Farm yesterday after reports that a giant, hairy, white creature had been seen bounding across the fields. A track of gigantic footprints could be clearly seen in the snow. The footprints led to the Vowel Forest, but then disappeared.

Footprints have been found in a few places, but there has only been one sighting of the abominable snowman.

"It is a mystery," said Officer Jewel from the local police.

READ AND DRAW

footprints going into some trees

CIRCLE THE CORRECT ANSWER

Is the abominable snowman small?

Yes or No

Were there handprints in the snow?

Yes or No

Was the abominable snowman seen?

Yes or No

Did the footprints go into the Vowel Forest?

Yes or No

What does a reporter do? ....

....

Why did Officer Jewel say that it was a mystery? ....

....

Find four words that mean *big*:

....

Cloud watching

Inky, Bee, and Snake were outside, sitting on the top of a hill. They were looking up at the big, fluffy clouds being blown along by the wind.

"That cloud looks like a house with windows," said Inky.

"And that one looks like a whale with a big, open mouth, swimming along in the sky," added Bee.

"Those clouds are all coming together to look like a dragon. There's the head, and those smaller, round clouds make a curving body and long tail," said Snake.

"And that one over there looks like a big cloud footprint. Even bigger than the abominable snowman's," he chuckled.

"I don't want to worry anyone, but look at those huge, gray clouds gathering in the distance!" said Bee. "I think perhaps it is time we headed home before we get wet."

Circle the correct answer

Were Inky, Bee, and Snake looking at the sea? ... Yes or No

Did a cloud look like Bee? ... Yes or No

Were the clouds pink? ... Yes or No

Did one of the clouds look like a footprint? ... Yes or No

What were Inky, Snake, and Bee doing?

....

....

What did Inky think the cloud looked like?

....

....

Why did Bee think they needed to go home?

....

....

What other things did they think the clouds looked like?

....

....

Monster verbs

Monsters flap and clap
When they're in a trap.

Monsters moan and groan
And then you find they've flown.

Monsters preen and clean
And after that they gleam!

Monsters shake and quake
When they're wide awake.

Monsters stomp and clomp
When they're in a swamp.

Monsters smash and crash
And then they have some mash.

Monsters fly and cry
High up in the sky!

Monsters howl and yowl
When they're on the prowl.

Monsters gnaw and roar
Then they're out the door.

Monsters hop and bop
And after that they stop!

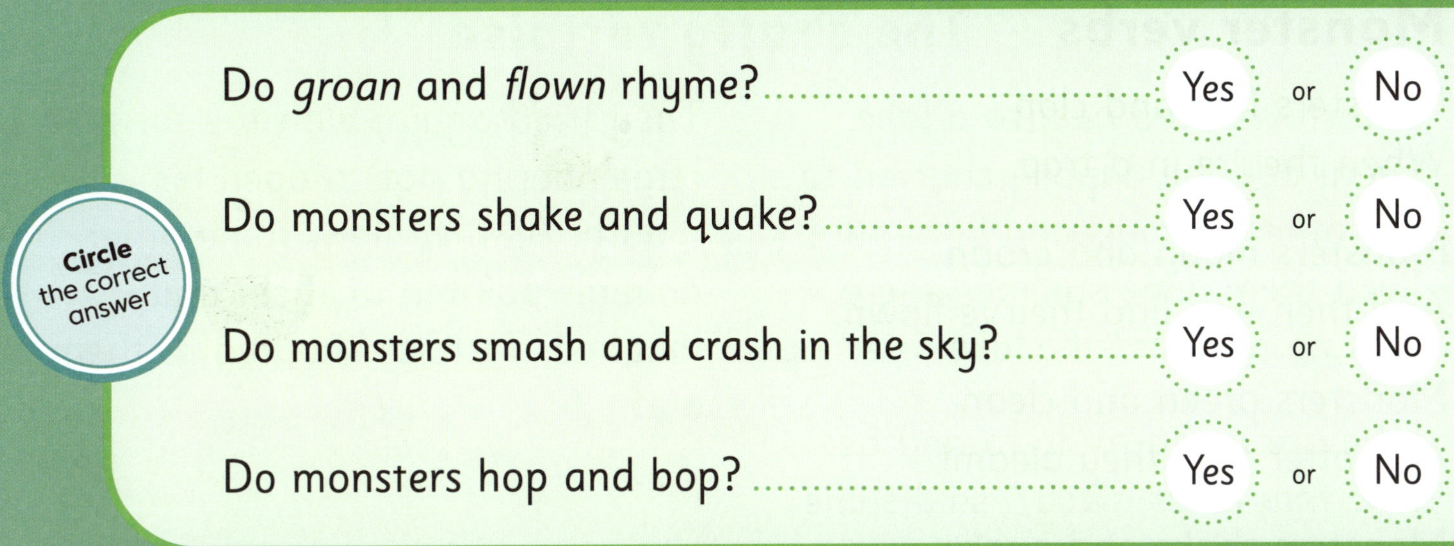

What do the monsters do when they're wide awake?

....

....

What do monsters do in a swamp?

....

....

Where are monsters when they fly and cry?

....

....

What does *gnaw* mean?

....

....

The chatty tortoise

A tortoise lived next to a lake. Every day, he happily chatted to the other animals and birds that lived there. One summer, there was no rain and the lake dried up.

"We are going to fly to another lake fifty miles away," said some geese.

"Fifty miles!" exclaimed the tortoise. "But I can only walk slowly." The geese offered to give the tortoise a lift.

"If you bite on to this stick we could carry you." Up they went. "Fantastic!" the tortoise shouted joyfully and...f
e
l
l!

They tried again, with the tortoise remembering not to open his mouth. As they flew, some other animals pointed at them and laughed. Tortoise shouted at them and...f
e
l
l
into a tree!

"You do look funny up there in that tree!" the animals laughed noisily. The tortoise was so upset he never spoke again.

Circle the correct answer

Did the tortoise live in a forest? .... Yes or No

Did the tortoise like talking? .... Yes or No

Did the tortoise climb on the back of a goose? ..... Yes or No

Did the tortoise land in a tree? .... Yes or No

Why were the animals leaving?

....

....

What did the geese use to carry the tortoise?

....

....

What happened when the tortoise spoke?

....

....

Why did the tortoise never talk again?

....

....

My best toy

"Now," announced Miss Beech to her class. "We have time for three more people to show us their favorite toys."

"My best toy is Mabel," Anna said. "She is a bunny and I was given her when I was two. She sleeps with me every night. My grandma knitted her a sweater and she has some other clothes as well."

Seth carefully took a model of a spaceship out of a box. "I like building things," he declared proudly. "I got this model as a present. I have to keep it up high because my baby brother can be very annoying. He tries to help but he destroys things instead."

"My best toys are my racing cars and track," said Hamid. "I have lots of cars and I enjoy making different tracks and racing my cars around them."

Activity 

Circle the correct answer

Is the teacher called Miss Smith? .... Yes or No

Is the word *favorite* an adjective? .... Yes or No

Is Mabel a toy rabbit? .... Yes or No

Does Seth like to build models? .... Yes or No

What are the children showing the rest of the class?

....

....

Why does Seth think his brother is annoying?

....

....

What does Hamid like doing?

....

....

What is your best toy?

....

....

Once Upon a Time Street

One morning, the delivery van arrived in Once Upon a Time Street. The driver went to deliver the boxes, but found that some of the address labels had rubbed off.

"I'll just have to read what's in the boxes and guess who they are for," he decided. He read the contents on the first box.

"A new wand, some featherlight wing spray, and forty bottles of assorted sparkle-dust. That will be for Fairy Godmother at number four."

"Three treasure maps, a box of telescope-cleaning wipes, and a sack of parrot food. Easy! Pirate Pete at number 40."

"Seashells, a rainbow comb, a songbook, and a comfy cushion. That will be Melody Mermaid at the end of the street."

"All done and sorted," said the driver, smiling as he drove off.

Circle the correct answer

Was it the evening? .... Yes or No

Does Fairy Godmother live at number four? .... Yes or No

Were there forty treasure maps? .... Yes or No

Did the driver sort all the boxes? .... Yes or No

Why didn't the delivery driver know where to deliver the boxes?

....

....

What pet does Pirate Pete have?

....

....

Why might the mermaid want a comfy cushion?

....

....

Why was the driver smiling when he drove off?

....

....

Jack and the Beanstalk

Jack and his mother lived in a small cottage. They were very poor. Jack's mother told him to take their cow to market to sell her.

After a while, a man walked by and started talking to Jack. "I will give you five magic beans for your cow," he said. "The beans will make you rich for the rest of your life."

Jack ran home and excitedly told his mother about the beans. "You silly boy!" she cried. "Five beans won't make us rich." She threw the beans out of the window.

Jack was cross with his mother but as it was nighttime, he would have to wait to find the beans. But when Jack went out the next morning there was a beanstalk growing up and up and into the clouds.

Circle the correct answer

Did Jack sell a horse? .... Yes or No

Did Jack get five magic beans? .... Yes or No

Was his mother very happy with Jack's deal? .... Yes or No

Did a giant sunflower grow in the garden? .... Yes or No

Why did they have to sell the cow?

....

....

Why was Jack excited about the beans?

....

....

What did his mother do with the beans?

....

....

What did Jack find in the garden the next morning?

....

....

Alice down the rabbit hole

Once upon a time, Alice saw a white rabbit run along and disappear down a rabbit hole.

She followed the rabbit, looked down, and tumbled into the hole! When Alice landed, she found herself in a hallway with lots of locked doors.

On a table was a key. The key didn't unlock any of the doors, but then Alice saw a tiny door down by her foot. The key fitted!

Alice lay down and peered through the door. She could see a fantastic garden.

When she stood up, there on the table was a bottle with a label on it that read: Drink me!

After Alice drank the whole bottle, a strange thing happened. Alice shrank and shrank until she was the size of a little doll!

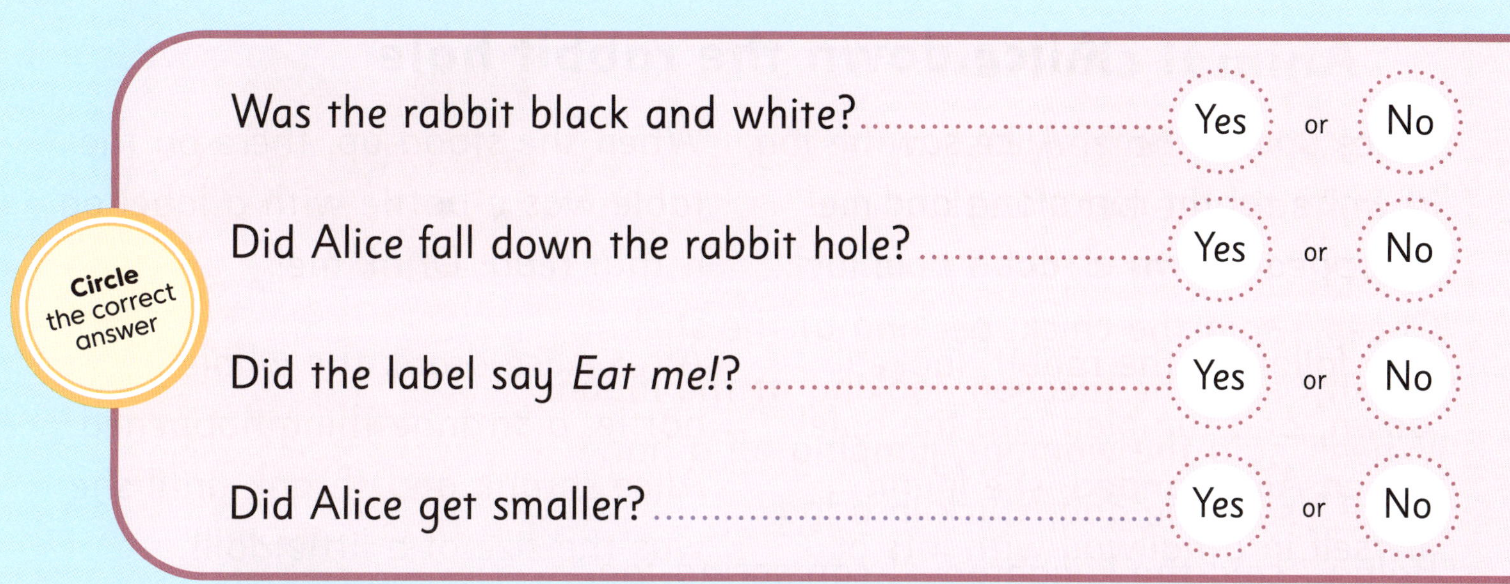

Why did Alice look down the rabbit hole?

....

....

Why couldn't she open the big doors?

....

....

What was written on the label on the bottle?

....

....

What happened when Alice drank from the bottle?

....

....

Animal chatter

"Croak," said the frog, lost in the fog.
"Buzz," said the bee. "Look at me!"
"Quack," said the duck. "I'm in luck."
"Cheep," said the chick, pecking at the stick.
"I wish," said the raccoon, looking at the moon.
"Whee!" said the wombat, jumping off a hat.
"Woof," said the dog, stuck in a log.
"Boing," said the kangaroo. "I can spring too."
"Ouch!" said the snail, out in the hail.
"Wow!" said the earwig. "You are big."
"Mmmm," said the skunk, sitting in the junk.
"Whoosh!" said the whale, flapping its tail.
"Twit-twoo," said the brown owl, out on the prowl.
"Growl," said the bear, from inside its lair.
"Moo," said the cow, as she gave a bow.
"Blob," said the fish, and had a wish.

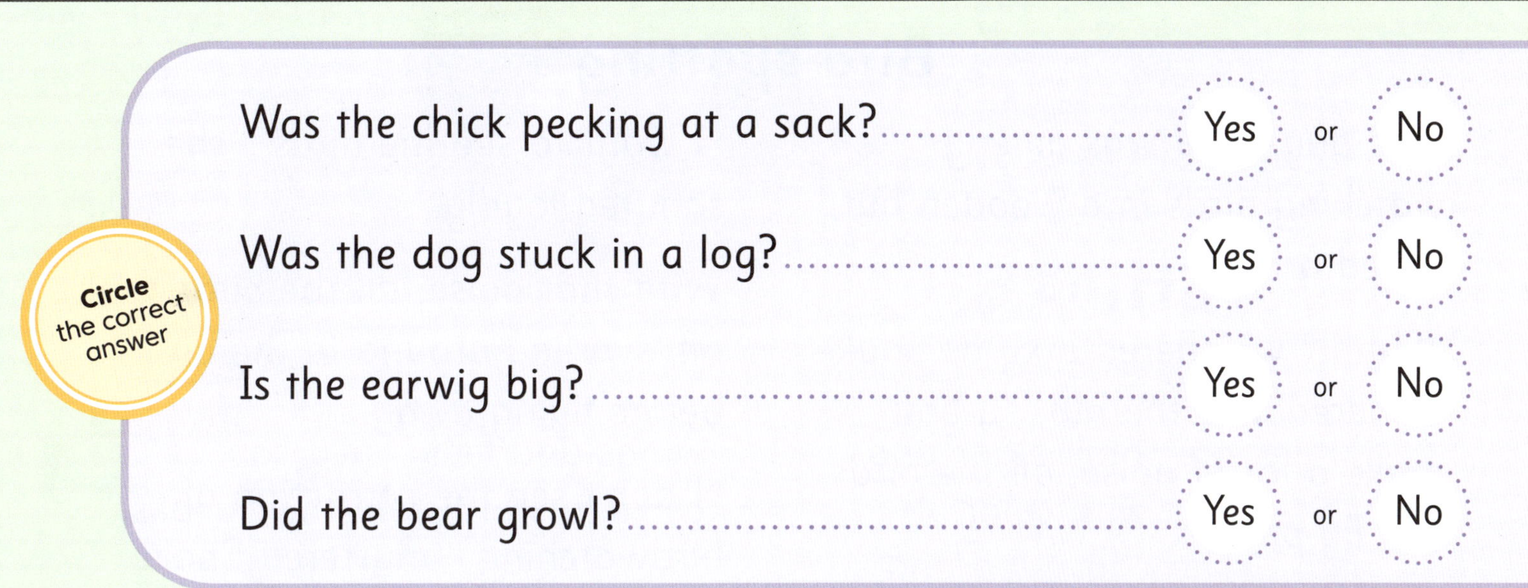

What was the wombat doing?

....

....

Why did the snail say *Ouch!*?

....

....

Which animal was flapping its tail?

....

....

What does *prowl* mean?

....

....

Bird spotting

One day, Inky was quietly watching birds in a wooden hut called a hide.

"Shhh!" whispered Inky as Snake slithered into the hut. "If you make a lot of noise, all the birds will fly off."

"What can you see?" murmured Snake quietly.

"Not much yet. But there are some mandarin ducks," replied Inky. "I've checked them off my spotter's list."

"Okay," said Snake slowly.

Just then a girl in a yellow shirt and green skirt ran up to the hide.

"I want to see the birds," she shouted loudly.

With that noise, all the birds took off, swirling around in the air before flying away.

"I don't see the attraction of birdwatching," muttered Snake. "Best thing about birds is they lay eggs. I like eggs," he mumbled.

"Well, I was hoping I might see my first bittern, but not with all this noise," sighed Inky. "Home time."

Circle the correct answer

Was Inky fishing? .... Yes or No

Did Inky spot mandarin ducks? .... Yes or No

Was the girl shouting? .... Yes or No

Is a bittern a bird? .... Yes or No

What was Inky doing?

....

....

Why did the birds fly away?

....

....

Does Snake like birdwatching?

....

....

What four words could replace *said*?

....

....

The enormous turnip

Arthur grew lots of vegetables in his garden. One of his turnips had grown enormous, so Arthur decided to pull up the turnip. He pulled and tugged and heaved, but the turnip did not move.

A nurse on her way home stopped to help Arthur. The two tried together, but the turnip did not move. A girl and her brother joined them, but their efforts were still no good.

Arthur's animals had been watching and they tried to help, too. His dog, with its purple collar, Arthur's turkey, his hen, and even his cat all got involved.

They all yanked and hauled and pulled and...

...suddenly the turnip shot out of the ground and all the people and animals tumbled into a heap!

To thank them all for their help and to help eat the turnip, Arthur invited everyone to dinner that evening.

Circle the correct answer

Did Arthur grow vegetables? .... Yes or No

Was the turnip very small? .... Yes or No

Did a doctor stop to help? .... Yes or No

Did Arthur's dog have a purple collar? .... Yes or No

Why did Arthur decide to pull up the turnip?

....

....

Why couldn't he pull it up?

....

....

Why did Arthur invite everyone who helped him to dinner?

....

....

Which four words in the story mean the same as *pulled*?

....

....

Dinosaur names

Dinosaurs lived millions of years ago, but they were not called dinosaurs until 1842, when the scientist Richard Owen named them. The word *dinosaur* means *monstrous* or *terrible lizard* in Greek and Latin. The *saur*, or *saurus*, part of the word means *lizard*.

Dinosaurs are often named after a characteristic they had, or where their fossils were found. Their names can be quite long and difficult to read, but a pronunciation guide can help you know how to say, or pronounce, difficult words. (Dictionaries often have pronunciation guides.)

The word *tyrannosaurus* is pronounced /t ie r a n oa s or u s/. *Tyrannosaurus* means *tyrant lizard* and *rex* means *king*. So *Tyrannosaurus rex* means *king of the tyrant lizards*.

Stegosaurus pronounced /s t e g oa s or u s/ means *roofed lizard*.

Lesothosaurus pronounced /l e s oa t oa s or u s/ means *lizard from Lesotho*.

Seismosaurus pronounced /s ie z m oa s or u s/ means *earth-shaking lizard*.

Circle the correct answer

Are any dinosaurs alive today? .... Yes or No

Does the word *dinosaur* mean *terrible lizard*? .... Yes or No

Is *Tyrannosaurus rex* a type of dinosaur? .... Yes or No

Does the word *rex* mean *princess*? .... Yes or No

What does the word *dinosaur* mean?

....

....

What does a pronunciation guide help people do?

....

....

What does the *stego* part mean in *stegosaurus*?

....

....

Why do you think a dinosaur was named *seismosaurus*?

....

....

Strawberry sundae

To make a strawberry sundae you will need:

- a punnet of strawberries
- 2 teaspoons of confectioners' sugar
- strawberry ice cream
- vanilla ice cream
- heavy whipping cream
- a small mint sprig and wafers (optional)

1. Crush three or four big strawberries with the confectioners' sugar to make a smooth strawberry sauce. Put this sauce in a bowl and chill in the fridge.
2. Cut the rest of the strawberries into halves or quarters. Save two halves.
3. Take the strawberry and the vanilla ice cream out of the freezer.
4. Layer scoops of the ice cream with layers of strawberries and the strawberry sauce in a tall sundae glass.
5. Top with the whipping cream and add the saved halved strawberry. If you want, add mint leaves and wafers.

Circle the correct answer

Is a sundae a type of cake? .... Yes or No

Is a strawberry sundae made with apples? .... Yes or No

Is ice cream an ingredient in a sundae? .... Yes or No

Is a sundae glass tall? .... Yes or No

How do you make strawberry sauce?

....

....

What sort of ice cream do you need to make a sundae?

....

....

What do you put in the sundae glass?

....

....

What could you top the sundae with?

....

....

Cut out these scenes, then try to reorder them to tell the story.

We hunted in rock pools.

We had lunch.

We made a sandcastle.

We went for a swim.

Cut out these scenes, then try to reorder them to tell the story.

There was a man
on the road.

The Sun made the man
feel hot.

The Wind blew on the man.

One day,
the Wind met the Sun.

The man
shrugged off his coat.

Cut out these illustrations, then try to reorder them to create the recipe.

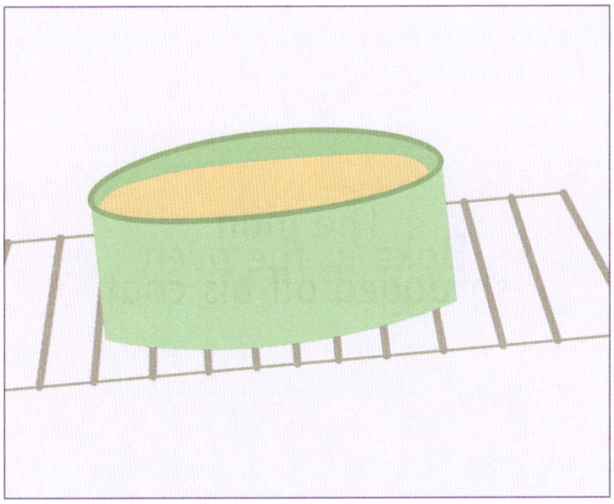

Add the butter to the bowl and mix everything.

Pour into a baking tin.

Weigh the ingredients.

Put the sugar, flour and baking powder in the bowl.

Break in the eggs.

Bake in the oven.